READY... SET...READ—AND LAUGH!

READY...
SET...READ—
AND LAUGH!

A FUNNY TREASURY FOR BEGINNING READERS

Compiled by **JOANNA COLE**
and **STEPHANIE CALMENSON**

A DOUBLEDAY BOOK
FOR YOUNG READERS

Published by Delacorte Press
Bantam Doubleday Dell Publishing Group, Inc.
1540 Broadway
New York, New York 10036

Library of Congress Cataloging-in-Publication Data

Ready...set...read—and laugh! : a funny treasury for beginning readers /
compiled by Joanna Cole and Stephanie Calmenson
   p. cm.
Companion to: Ready...set...read!
Includes index.
Summary: A collection of humorous stories, poems, riddles and the like for beginning readers.
ISBN 0-385-32119-8
1. Children's literature. [1. Literature—Collections. 2. Humorous stories. 3. Humorous poetry.]
I. Cole, Joanna. II. Calmenson, Stephanie.
PZ5.R19893   1995   94-32535   CIP   AC

The text of this book is set in Adobe Garamond and ITC Kabel.
Art Direction by Diana Klemin
Book Design by David November & Co., Inc.
R. L. 2.O
Manufactured in the United States of America
September 1995

ACKNOWLEDGMENTS

Grateful acknowledgment is made for permission to reprint the following:

Stephanie Calmenson. "Weather Report" by Stephanie Calmenson. Copyright © 1995 by Stephanie Calmenson. Used by permission of the author.

Joanna Cole. "The Mail Box Poem" by Joanna Cole. Copyright © 1995 by Joanna Cole. Used by permission of the author.

Joanna Cole and Philip Cole. "Bigger and Smaller," adapted from *Big Goof and Little Goof* by Joanna Cole and Philip Cole, illustrated by M. K. Brown. Text copyright © 1989 by Joanna and Philip Cole; illustrations copyright © 1989 by M. K. Brown. Reprinted by permission of Scholastic Inc.

Lee Bennett Hopkins. "This Tooth" by Lee Bennett Hopkins from *More Surprises,* ed. by Lee Bennett Hopkins. Copyright © 1987 by Lee Bennett Hopkins. Reprinted by permission of HarperCollins Publishers.

Bobbi Katz. "Morning" by Bobbi Katz from *Upside Down and Inside Out.* Copyright © 1973. Wordsong Books, Boyds Mills Press. Reprinted by permission of the author.

Karla Kuskin. "Bugs" from *Dogs & Dragons, Trees & Dreams* by Karla Kuskin. Copyright © 1980 by Karla Kuskin. Reprinted by permission of HarperCollins Publishers.

Myra Cohn Livingston. "At the Zoo" from *A Song I Sang to You* by Myra Cohn Livingston. Copyright © 1984, 1969, 1967, 1965, 1959, 1958 by Myra Cohn Livingston. All copyrights have been renewed. Published by Harcourt Brace. Reprinted by permission of Marian Reiner for the author.

Arnold Lobel. "Boom! Boom!" from *Whiskers and Rhymes* by Arnold Lobel. Copyright © 1985 by Arnold Lobel. By permission of Greenwillow Books, a division of William Morrow & Company, Inc.

James Marshall. "Pizza Time" from *Fox on the Job* by James Marshall. Copyright © 1988 by James Marshall. Used by permission of Dial Books for Young Readers, a division of Penguin Books USA Inc.

Eve Merriam. "The Birthday Cow" from *The Birthday Cow* by Eve Merriam. Copyright © 1978 by Eve Merriam. Reprinted by permission of Marian Reiner.

Peggy Parish. *Come Back, Amelia Bedelia* by Peggy Parish, illustrated by Wallace Tripp. Text copyright © 1971 by Peggy Parish. Illustrations copyright © 1971 by Wallace Tripp. Reprinted by permission of HarperCollins Publishers.

Jack Prelutsky. "Spaghetti! Spaghetti!" from *Rainy Rainy Saturday* by Jack Prelutsky. Copyright © 1980 by Jack Prelutsky. By permission of Greenwillow Books, a division of William Morrow & Company, Inc.

Maurice Sendak. "March" from *Chicken Soup with Rice: A Book of Months* by Maurice Sendak. Copyright © 1962 by Maurice Sendak. Reprinted by permission of HarperCollins Publishers.

Dr. Seuss. "Rain Storm" from *Oh Say Can You Say?* by Dr. Seuss™ and copyright © 1979 by Dr. Seuss Enterprises, L.P. Reprinted by permission of Random House, Inc.

Nancy Shaw. Abridged from *Sheep in a Shop* by Nancy Shaw. Text copyright © 1991 by Nancy Shaw. Illustrations copyright © 1991 by Margot Apple. Reprinted by permission of Houghton Mifflin Co. All rights reserved.

William Jay Smith. "People" from *Laughing Time* by William Jay Smith. Copyright © 1990 by William Jay Smith. Reprinted by permission of Farrar, Straus & Giroux, Inc.

Bernard Wiseman. "The Riddles" from *Morris and Boris, Three Stories* by Bernard Wiseman. Dodd, Mead, 1974. Reprinted by permission of the author.

To Christopher, Bartley, Michael,
Meghan, Ian, Lauren, Sara, Anna, Elana,
Camilla, Devin, Caitlin.

– J.C. and S.C.

CONTENTS

STORIES

A birthday's coming! Hip hooray!

Five sheep shop for the big, big day.

Sheep find rackets. Sheep find rockets.

Sheep find jackets full of pockets.

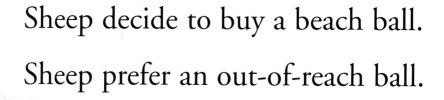

Sheep decide to buy a beach ball.

Sheep prefer an out-of-reach ball.

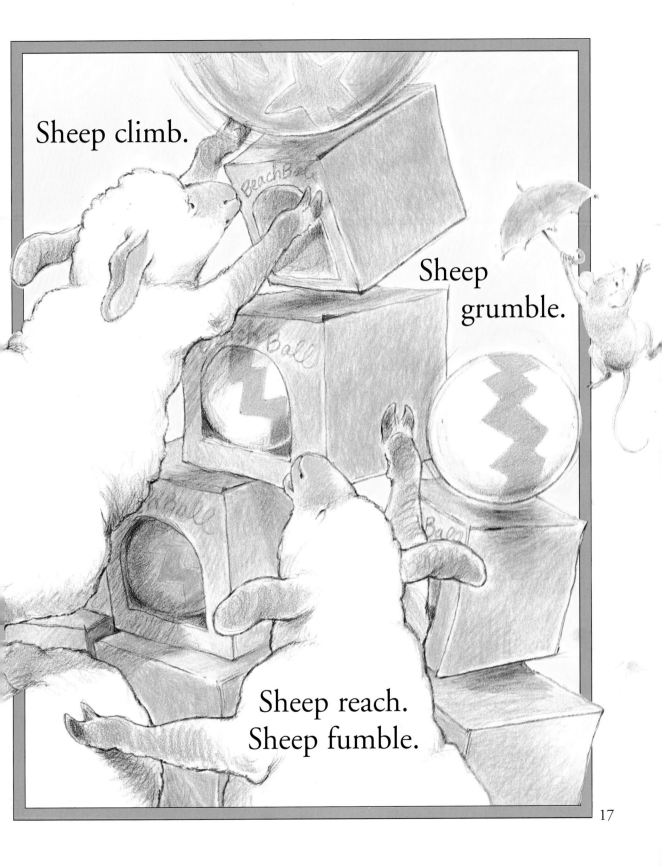

Sheep climb.

Sheep
grumble.

Sheep reach.
Sheep fumble.

17

Sheep sprawl.

Boxes tumble.

Boxes fall in one big jumble.

Sheep put back the beach ball stack.
They choose some ribbon
from the rack.

21

They dump their bank. Pennies clank.

There's not enough to buy this stuff.

Sheep blink. Sheep think.

What can they swap to pay the shop?

Sheep clip wool, three bags full.

Sheep trade.

The bill is paid.

Sheep hop home

in the warm spring sun.

They're ready for some birthday fun.

BIGGER AND SMALLER

by Joanna and Philip Cole
Illustrated by M. K. Brown
from Big Goof and Little Goof

One night, Big Goof and Little Goof were
watching TV. The TV lady said, "If you do
not get enough sleep, you will get sick."
"Oh no!" said Big Goof. "Look how late it is!"
"We'd better go to bed right away!" said
Little Goof.

The two Goofs were in a big hurry. They took off their shoes. They took off their pants. They took off their shirts. They threw their clothes all over the place. Then they jumped into bed and went right to sleep.

Very early the next morning, while it was still dark, a car honked outside.

The two Goofs were so sleepy, they could hardly open their eyes.

They found clothes and began to put them on.

Big Goof looked down. "I must be getting bigger!" he cried. "I am too big for my clothes."

"Look at *me*!" cried Little Goof. "I am getting *smaller*! I am too small for my clothes!"

"This is terrible," said Big Goof.

"I was *already* big."

34

"And I was already little," said Little Goof.

"I will be too big to sit in my chair," said
Big Goof.
"I will be too little to sit in mine," said
Little Goof.

"We will get tired
from standing
up all the time!"

"That TV lady was right," Big Goof said.

"We did not get enough sleep, and we got sick."

"I got Getting-Bigger sickness," said Big Goof.

"I got Getting-Smaller sickness!" said
Little Goof.

"If we are sick,
we ought to be in bed."

Slowly, slowly, the two Goofs took off
their shoes. They took off their pants.
They took off their shirts. They folded their
clothes neatly, got into bed, and went to sleep.

Later that same morning, when the sun
was shining brightly, a car honked outside.
The Goofs woke up. This time they were not
sleepy. Their eyes were wide open.

They put on
their clothes the
right way.

"Look what
happened!"
said Little Goof.

"That TV lady was sure smart. All that sleep made us the right size again," said Big Goof.

Just look at those Goofs now.

Isn't it wonderful to see them

all better and back to normal?

PIZZA TIME
by James Marshall
from Fox on the Job

Fox saw his friend Dexter coming out of the pizza parlor.

"You can't fire *me*," said Dexter.

"I quit!"

"Fine," said the boss. "Maybe my next delivery boy won't eat up all the pizza!"

Dexter left in a huff. And Fox stepped inside the pizza parlor.

"Do you have a job for me?" asked Fox.

"Do you like pizza?" said the boss.

"I prefer hot dogs," said Fox.

"Excellent," said the boss. "Are you fast on your feet?"

"Like the wind," said Fox.

"Excellent," said the boss.

"Take this pizza over to Mrs. O'Hara.

She has been waiting a long time."

Fox was out the door in a flash.

On Homer's Hill Fox picked up speed.

"I'm the fastest fox in town," he said.

At that moment Louise came around

the corner. She was taking her pet mice

to the vet for their shots.

It was quite a crash!

Fox, Louise, and everything else
went flying.

They saw stars.

"Now you've done it!" said Fox.

"You've made me late.

I'll really have to step on it!"

And he hurried away.

Louise went to the vet's.

Doctor Jane opened the box.

"Where are your pet mice?" she said.

"This looks like a pizza."

"Uh-oh," said Louise.

Fox knocked on Mrs. O'Hara's door.

"It's about time," said Mrs. O'Hara.

"I'm having a party.

And we're just dying for pizza."

"It will be worth the wait," said Fox.

"Pizza time!" said Mrs. O'Hara to
her friends. She opened the box.

Back at the pizza parlor the boss was hopping mad.

"Mrs. O'Hara just called," he said.

"And you are fired!"

"Didn't she like the pizza?" said Fox.

Boris the Bear met Morris the Moose.

"Do you like riddles?" Boris asked.

Morris asked, "How do they taste?"

Boris said, "You do not eat riddles."

Morris asked, "Do you drink them?"

Boris said, "You do not eat riddles.

You do not drink riddles. You ask them!

Listen—I will ask you a riddle."

Boris asked, "What has four feet—"

Morris yelled, "ME!"

"I did not finish," Boris said.

"What has four feet and a tail—"

"ME!" Morris yelled.

"I still did not finish!" Boris cried.

"Let me finish!"

Morris put a hoof over his mouth.

Boris asked, "What has four feet and

a tail and flies?"

"ME!" Morris yelled. "I have four feet and a tail, and flies come and sit on me all the time!"

"No, no!" Boris growled.

"The answer is: A horse in an airplane!

"Here is another riddle. What kind of comb cannot comb hair?"

"I know!" Morris cried.

"A broken comb!"

"NO! NO! NO!" Boris shouted.

"The answer is a honeycomb!"

"What is a honeycomb?" Morris asked.

Boris said, "It is the inside of a bee house.

Don't you know anything?"

Morris said, "I know about riddles.
You do not eat riddles. You do not drink
riddles. You ASK riddles."

Boris said, "And you must answer them!

Try to answer this riddle.

What kind of bee does not sting?"

"I know!" cried Morris. "A friendly bee!"

"NO! NO!" Boris yelled.

Morris cried, "A sleeping bee!"

"NO! NO! NO!" Boris shouted.

"The answer is: a beetle. Oh, you don't

know how to answer riddles. I am

not going to ask you any more."

Morris said, "You know how to answer riddles. Let me ask you riddles."

"Go ahead," said Boris. "Ask me riddles."

Morris asked, "What has four feet and a tail and flies?"

Boris answered, "A horse in an airplane."
"No! No!" Morris cried. "A moose in an airplane!"

Boris yelled, "You mean a HORSE!" Morris said, "I mean a moose. I want a moose to get an airplane ride!"

Then Morris said, "Here is another riddle.
What kind of beetle does not sting?"
Boris said, "You mean, what kind of
BEE does not sting!"

Morris laughed. "I mean what kind of
beetle! All bees sting!"

Boris shouted, "Oh, you don't know anything about riddles! I am going home!"

A bird asked Morris, "What is he angry about?"

"Riddles," said Morris. "He does not like them."

COME BACK, AMELIA BEDELIA

by Peggy Parish
Pictures by Wallace Tripp

"Oh, my cream puffs!" said Amelia Bedelia. She
went to the stove.

"Just right," she said. Amelia Bedelia took her
cream puffs out of the stove.

"There now," she said. "I'll just let them cool. Then
I will fill them with chocolate cream."

Mrs. Rogers came into the kitchen.

"Good morning, Amelia Bedelia," she said.

"Good morning," said Amelia Bedelia.

"I will have some cereal with my coffee this morning," said Mrs. Rogers.

"All right," said Amelia Bedelia.

Mrs. Rogers went into the dining room.

Amelia Bedelia got the cereal. She put some in a cup. And she fixed Mrs. Rogers some cereal with her coffee. She took it into the dining room.

"Amelia Bedelia!" said Mrs. Rogers. "What is this mess?"

"It's your cereal with coffee," said Amelia Bedelia.

"Oh, you are impossible!" said Mrs. Rogers. "You're fired!"

"You mean you don't want me anymore?" asked Amelia Bedelia.

"That is just what I mean," said Mrs. Rogers. "Now go!"

Amelia Bedelia got her bag. And she went away.

Amelia Bedelia walked toward town.

"Now what will I do?" she asked. She passed by the beauty shop. A sign said LADY WANTED.

"Now let's see what that's about," said Amelia Bedelia. She went into the beauty shop.

"Can I help you?"
asked a lady.

"No, I came
to help you," said Amelia Bedelia.

"Can you fix hair?" asked
the lady.

"Oh yes," said Amelia
Bedelia. "I can do that."

"Then you can start now,"
said the lady. "Mrs.
Hewes is waiting to have
her hair pinned up."

"All right," said Amelia Bedelia. She looked all around.

"But I don't see any pins," she thought. "It's a good thing I carry some with me."

Amelia Bedelia opened her purse. She took out some pins. And Amelia Bedelia began to pin up Mrs. Hewes' hair.

"What are you doing?" said Mrs. Hewes.

"Pinning up your hair," said Amelia Bedelia. "Did I stick you?"

"Help!" called Mrs. Hewes.

"Oh, no!" she said. "What have you done? Go away right this minute."

"All right," said Amelia Bedelia.

So Amelia Bedelia went on her way.

"Now why did she get so mad?" asked Amelia Bedelia. "I just did what she told me to do."

Amelia Bedelia looked in all the stores. She came to
a dress shop. It had a HELP WANTED sign in the window.
Amelia Bedelia went into the store.

"What kind of help is wanted?" she asked.

"Sewing help," said the lady. "Can you sew?"

"Yes," said Amelia Bedelia. "I am very handy with a needle." "Then come with me," said the lady.

She took Amelia Bedelia into a back room.

"Please shorten these dresses. They are already marked," said the lady.

"All right," said Amelia Bedelia. The lady left her.

"I don't need to sew to do this," said Amelia Bedelia.

She took the scissors. And Amelia Bedelia shortened those dresses.

Amelia Bedelia went back to the front of the store.

"I'm finished," she said. "What is next?"

"Finished!" said the lady. "How could you be?"

The lady went into the back room. She saw the dresses.

"Oh, no!" she said. "You have ruined them!"

"But I just shortened them," said Amelia Bedelia.

"Go away," said the lady. "I don't want you."

So Amelia Bedelia went.

"Some folks," she said, "I just don't understand them."

Amelia Bedelia walked another block or so. She saw a sign in a window. It said FILE CLERK WANTED.

"Now I wonder what a file clerk is," she said. "I'll just go in and find out."

A man met her. "Are you a file clerk?" he asked.

"I will be one," said Amelia Bedelia, "if you will tell me what to do."

"All right," said the man. "First, take these letters. They need stamps. Then file these papers."

"I'll do that," said Amelia Bedelia.

The man went into his office. Amelia Bedelia took each letter. She put it on the floor. And Amelia Bedelia stamped on it. "There," she said. "That should be enough stamps.

Now I better
get these papers filed."

Amelia Bedelia looked at the papers. Then she looked in her purse. She found a fingernail file.

"It sure is small to file all these papers. But I will do the best I can." And Amelia Bedelia began to file the papers.

The man came back. "Stop!" he said. "What are you doing?"

"Just filing your papers," said Amelia Bedelia. "Do
you have a bigger file?"

"Oh, no!" said the man. "Do go away."

So Amelia Bedelia went.

"I declare!" she said. "Everybody is mad today."

Amelia Bedelia walked on down the street. She came to a doctor's office. There was a sign that said HELP WANTED.

"Maybe that's the job for me," said Amelia Bedelia. She went inside. The doctor was there.

"I will be your help," said Amelia Bedelia.

"Good," said the doctor. "Bring in the patients one at a time. Come when I buzz for you."

"All right," said Amelia Bedelia. "I can do that." The doctor went into his office.

A woman
and a girl
came in.

"Who is
the patient?"
asked Amelia
Bedelia.

"Jane," said
the woman.

"Then I'll
take her in,"
said Amelia
Bedelia. She
picked Jane up.

"Put me down! I can walk!" screamed Jane.

"Nope," said Amelia Bedelia, "the doctor said to
bring you in." And Amelia Bedelia carried Jane into
the doctor's office.

"Put Jane down!" said the doctor.

Amelia Bedelia went back to her desk. A little later the buzzer rang.

"I need your help," said the doctor. "Dickie has a bad cut. He needs a few stitches."

"I can take care of that," said Amelia Bedelia. She opened her purse. "Here is a needle. Now, what color thread does Dickie like?"

"No! No!" said the doctor. "I wanted you to put my gloves on. Can you do that?"

"Oh my, yes!" said Amelia Bedelia. "I will be glad to." So Amelia Bedelia put the doctor's gloves on.

"There now," she said. "They're a little big, but they're on. What next?"

The doctor looked at Amelia Bedelia. His face turned red.

"Go home!" he said.

"Home!" said Amelia Bedelia. "My goodness! I forgot about my cream puffs. I must go back and fill them."

Amelia
Bedelia
went back
to the
Rogers'
house.

"I'll just
make the
chocolate
cream,"
said Amelia Bedelia.

She put a little of this and bit of that into a pot. She mixed and she stirred. And soon her chocolate cream was cooked.

Mrs. Rogers came into the kitchen. "That smells good," she said.

"Well," said Amelia Bedelia, "I'll just fill the cream puffs. Then I will be on my way."

"Oh, no!" said Mrs. Rogers. "I'm sorry I got mad. Please come back, Amelia Bedelia, we miss you."

"All right," said Amelia Bedelia. "I will be glad to."

Mr. Rogers came into the kitchen.

"I'm hungry," he said. Amelia Bedelia, please heat me a can of soup."

"All right," said Amelia Bedelia.

She took a can of soup. She put it in a pot. And Amelia Bedelia heated that can of soup.

POEMS

Illustrated by

MELISSA SWEET

Bugs
by Karla Kuskin

I am very fond of bugs.

I kiss them

And I give them hugs.

THE BIRTHDAY COW

by Eve Merriam

Happy Mooday to you,

Happy Mooday to you.

Happy Mooday,

Dear Youday.

Happy Mooday to you.

At the Zoo

by Myra Cohn Livingston

I've been to the zoo

where the thing that you do

is watching the things

that the animals do —

and watching

the animals

all watching

you!

PEOPLE
by William Jay Smith

Hour after hour,

In many places,

People sit,

Making faces.

THIS TOOTH
by Lee Bennett Hopkins

I jiggled it

jaggled it

jerked it.

I pushed

and pulled

and poked it.

But —

As soon as I stopped,

and left it alone,

This tooth came out

on its very own.

THE MAILBOX POEM

by Joanna Cole

I wanted to visit Grandma.

I missed her smiling face.

But I didn't have the plane fare

To travel to her place.

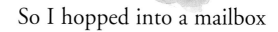

So I hopped into a mailbox

With a stamp and her address.

That's how I got to Grandma's

By Next-Day Express!

SPAGHETTI! SPAGHETTI!

by Jack Prelutsky

Spaghetti! spaghetti!

you're wonderful stuff,

I love you, spaghetti,

I can't get enough.

You're covered with sauce

and you're sprinkled with cheese,

spaghetti! spaghetti!

oh, give me some please.

Spaghetti! spaghetti!

piled high in a mound,

you wiggle, you wriggle,

you squiggle around.

There's slurpy spaghetti

all over my plate,

spaghetti! spaghetti!

I think you are great.

Spaghetti! spaghetti!

I love you a lot,

you're slishy, you're sloshy,

delicious and hot.

I gobble you down,

oh, I can't get enough,

spaghetti! spaghetti!

you're wonderful stuff.

I Made a Mistake

Author unknown

I went upstairs to make my bed.

I made a mistake and bumped my head.

I went downstairs to wash the dishes.

I made a mistake and washed the fishes.

I went in the kitchen to bake a pie.

I made a mistake and baked a fly.

I went outside to hang the clothes.

I made a mistake and hung my nose.

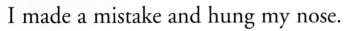

HELLO, BILL
Author unknown

"Hello, Bill."

"Where are you going, Bill?"

"Downtown, Bill."

"What for, Bill?"

"To pay my gas bill."

"How much, Bill?"

"A ten-dollar bill."

"So long, Bill."

BOOM! BOOM!
by Arnold Lobel

Boom! Boom!

My feet are large.

Each shoe is like a garbage barge.

Boom! Boom!

My poor head aches.

Wherever I step, the sidewalk breaks.

WEATHER REPORT

by Stephanie Calmenson

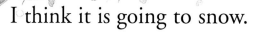

I think it is going to snow.

But it's getting warm — oh no!

Here comes the wind and rain.

There may be a hurricane!

Now the clouds are on the run.

Look at the sky — there's the sun!

(Isn't weather reporting fun?)

RAIN STORM

Written and Illustrated by Dr. Seuss

The storm starts

when the drops start dropping.

When the drops stop dropping

then the storm starts stopping.

MARCH

Written and illustrated
by Maurice Sendak
from Chicken Soup with Rice: A Book of Months

In March the wind

blows down the door

and spills my soup

upon the floor.

It laps it up

and roars for more.

Blowing once

blowing twice

blowing chicken soup

with rice.

MORNING
by Bobbi Katz

It's morning in the afternoon.

So eat your bacon with a spoon.

And if you have a scrambled egg,

you could feed it to your leg.

Then drink your milk up with your nose

and hop right into Daddy's clothes.

Put your left shoe on your right.

It's time to start the day.

Good night!

FUN AND GAMES

Compiled by **JOANNA COLE**

and **STEPHANIE CALMENSON**

Illustrated by **CHRIS DEMAREST**

What is the best day to cook eggs?

Fry-day.

What is the best way to call a mean,

green, hairy monster?

Long distance.

What keys do not open doors?

Monkeys.

What has four legs and a tail

and goes tick-tock?

A watchdog.

What animal are you like

when you take a bath?

A little bear.

What goes ABCD . . . *slurp!*

A person eating alphabet soup.

What did the sad ghost say?

"Boo-hoo!"

What did the big balloon say

to the small balloon?

My pop is bigger than your pop.

What letter is a question?

Y.

What letter is a green vegetable?

P.

What letter is wet and blue?

C.

What has a pen,

but no ink?

A pig.

What has six legs,

but walks on four feet?

A horse with a rider.

When you look at my face,

you see somebody.

When you look at my back,

you see nobody.

What am I?

A mirror.

The more

you take from me,

the bigger I get.

What am I?

A hole.

Knock-knock.

Who's there?

Orange.

Orange who?

Orange you glad

to see me?

Knock-knock.

Who's there?

Lettuce.

Lettuce who?

Lettuce go out tonight.

Knock-knock.

Who's there?

Ken.

Ken who?

Ken you come out

and play?

WE CAN FLY!
A Rebus Story

This . She

 an .

This , **2**.

He does  have an .

The goes up in the .

The goes up in the 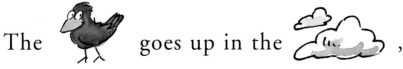, **2**.

The  goes over a . The

goes over a , 2 . The goes

over a . The goes

over a , 2 . The gets

-d. The does

get -d. The 's a new way

to !

Thanks for the ride!

Look who wrote a book about

clowns — someone named U. R. Funny!

We think something funny

is going on at Betty's Book Shop.

Don't you?

1 day, 👁 had **2** go **2** the

🏪 STORE . 👁 had **2** buy 🥚 .

👁 went down-⬜ . But 👁

4-got my 🔑 ! 👁 went

up-⬜ . 👁 got my 🔑 .

👁 went down-⬜ .

But  4-got my .

went up- . got my

. went down- .

But 4-got my .

went up-

guess what did next?

DO YOUR EARS HANG LOW?
A Song to Sing and Read

Do your ears hang low?___ Do they wob-ble to and

fro? Can you tie them in a knot? Can you tie them in a

bow? Can you throw them o-ver your shoul-der like a con-ti-nent-al

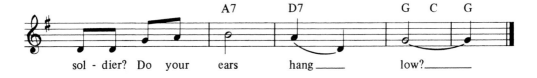

sol-dier? Do your ears hang ___ low? ___

THE DINOSAUR BONE
A Rebus Story

A  was looking    .

She looked under   .

She looked under   .

But she did    any  .

Then the  a .

136

She went in-2 the [cave] . She turned

on her [flashlight] . "There's my [bone] !"

said the [explorer] . " O no! It's my [bone] !"

said a [dinosaur] .

Tell this story to a friend,

but make sure you have plenty of time!

Jill and Bill had a cow.

Every day the cow gave milk.

Every day the cow also

mooed very loudly.

"That cow is too noisy!"

said Jill.

"Let's give her away,"

said Bill.

So they gave the cow away.

"Now it is nice and quiet,"

said Bill. "But we have no milk."

"Let's get the cow back,"

said Jill.

So they got the cow back.

"Now we have lots of milk,"

said Jill. "But it is too noisy!"

"Let's give the cow away,"

said Bill.

So they gave the cow away.

"Now it is nice and quiet,"

said Bill. "But we have no milk."

"Let's get the cow back,"

said Jill.

And so on, and so on, and so on . . .

TITLE INDEX

AUTHOR AND ARTIST INDEX

Joanna Cole

is the author of many highly praised children's books, including *The Magic School Bus*™ series. She lives in Connecticut.

Stephanie Calmenson

is the author of numerous popular books for children, including *The Principal's New Clothes*. She lives in New York.

Together, Cole and Calmenson

have compiled several best-selling anthologies, including, for Doubleday, *The Read-Aloud Treasury, Ready…Set…Read!*, and *The Laugh Book*.